Introduction to Cabochon Cutting and the Lapidary Hobby

by
Dick Friesen

Front Cover
Some finished gemstones.
Back Cover
Photo: Dick Friesen
Bio: Andrea Rodriguez

Introduction to Cabochon Cutting and the Lapidary Hobby

Written by
Dick Friesen
787 Joyce St.
Livermore, CA 94550

ISBN-13: 978-1514255360
ISBN-10: 1514255367

Notice of Liability

Introduction

This book is intended to be a guide for the beginner in the art of cabochon cutting and a brief overview of the lapidary hobby. No attempt is made to present all of the views on the various steps in the cutting, sanding, and polishing process. The steps described here are those used by the author to instruct beginners in his shop and have been refined by 20 years of cutting for both the hobby and commercial fields.

The Equipment

There are five types of power equipment used in amateur cabochon (cab) making: slab saw, trim saw, grinder, sander, and polisher. There are, however, many different types or models of each.

Slab Saw
Slab saws are used for cutting rough rock into slabs for cabs. They are also used to cut rough rock into shapes for bookends, intarsia, jewelry boxes, etc. Slab saws use a large (10" to 36" diameter) diamond blade in an oil or water bath to cut rock. The rock is held in a vise and fed into the blade by lead screw or gravity. There is usually a cutoff switch at the end of the cut. An easy way to clean the oil from slabs is by covering the slab with "kitty litter".

Trim Saw
Trim saws are used to cut the slabs into a rough outline of the final shape desired. They are similar to the slab saws but use a smaller diamond blade (4" to 10") and some have small clamps to allow slabbing of small rocks. The slabs are hand held and the clamps are usually hand fed. Almost all older saws use oil as the cutting lubricant while the newer saws use water to which a wetting agent is frequently added. The blades are available in several different widths from .004" to .035" with the thinner blades generally used on more valuable material such as opal.

Grinder

Grinders are used to shape the rough outline of the cab from the trim saw into the final shape and size desired for the cab. Grinders may be 4" to 8" drums or flat wheels and may be silicon carbide or diamond. The cab is hand held and almost all grinders use water as the cooler and lubricant.

Sander

Sanders are used to remove the grinding scratches and to pre-polish the cab. Like grinders they may be 4" to 8" drums or flat wheels and may be silicon carbide or diamond. The most common sanders are 6" or 8" expandable drums that can use either silicon carbide or diamond belts. There are also some inexpensive 6" or 8" flat wheel sanders that use adhesive backed diamond disks.

Polisher

Polishers are used to put the final shine or polish on the cab. They are usually 6" or 8" diameter disks with a leather disk that has the polishing compound applied to it as the wheel turns. The compound is usually tin or cerium oxide, one of several commercial polishing compounds, or diamond.

Dop Wax Heater

The wax that is used to hold the stone to a wooden stick (dop stick) is called dop wax. It is a hard wax at room temperature and is heated to soften it to a very thick paste. The heater may be a piece of commercial equipment, a common kitchen hot plate, an alcohol lamp, or some other heat source.

Other Equipment

There are a few other types of equipment that are in common use in the hobby. Flat sanders are used to sand large flats for use in book ends, display slabs, jewelry boxes, lamps, and intarsia. Wood sanders were popular at one time but are not used much now. They used diamond compound applied to wooden drums. Tumblers are used to polish small stones. Rotary tumblers are relatively inexpensive and are frequently the first equipment used by the beginner. Vibrating tumblers are more expensive but polish stones much faster.

Diamond vs. Carborundum

The question always comes up: which is better diamond or carborundum (silicon carbide)? The answer is diamond is faster, silicon carbide is cheaper. If you can afford diamond you will like it better but if you are cutting agate or softer stones (and that is what most everyone cuts) there is nothing you can not grind, sand, and polish with silicon carbide.

If you plan to cut sapphires or harder stones the wear rate on silicon carbide is so high that diamond is the only practical answer. In addition to speed, silicon carbide requires more care to get the same results. Silicon carbide belts wear enough that a used 400 grit may be finer than a newer 600. The life of the belts is enough shorter that most people are willing to pay the extra money.

Diamond grinding wheels require a true running arbor. Grinding cabs and especially larger rocks on a diamond wheel that has play in it can hammer the diamonds loose from the surface. Silicon carbide is more tolerant of a small amount of hammering and, since they need to be trued up with a dressing tool to keep the surface flat anyway, the dressing process can remove a small amount of runout.

Safety

The lapidary hobby is relatively safe but there are a few areas where accidents could happen. Always use safety glasses when cutting on the trim saw. The saw cuts fast enough to send chips flying. The heater to warm the cab to be dopped is sometimes an alcohol lamp with an open flame, keep your fingers and flammable items away. Never grind or sand anything dry. Dry sanding is recommended for some stones but until you know which stones are safe it is not worth the risk. Dry sanding raises a lot of dust and the possibility of adverse effects from exposure to, or breathing this dust is too high to justify it. Wet sanding holds the dust in the water and it is not much of a health hazard. The grinding and sanding wheels are all smooth enough to present no hazard to your fingers, however, the grinding wheels can do a number on your fingernails and sometimes the edges are sharp enough to give you a cut similar to a paper cut. Just keep your fingers away.

Step 1: Marking and Sawing the Cab

Cutting a Slab

Unless you belong to a club that has a slab saw, you have a friend that has a slab saw, or just feel like spending a lot of money ($2000 up) the best place to start is by buying your slabs. They are available at most rock shops and gem and mineral shows. If you have a rough rock that you would like to cut, save it until you have more experience. Unless you are very lucky most rocks that are collected by beginners will have characteristics, hardness, fractures, undercutting, etc.. that make them unsuitable for your first cabs.

Marking the Slab

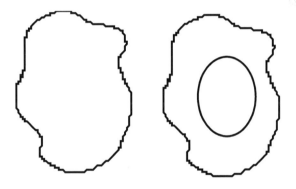

Using a cab outline template find the place on the slab you want to use as your cab. Using a sharpened aluminum rod or permanent marking pen, outline the cab on the back of the slab. Resist the temptation to mark the front or top of the slab. It is difficult to avoid cutting the cab too small when it is marked on top. Choose a slab that has a pattern that will allow small misplacement of the template on the back side, later you can find special two sided templates to allow precise marking.

Marking Trim Lines

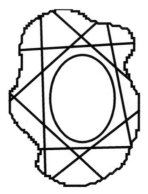

Using a sharpened aluminum rod or marking pen, mark trim lines on the slab. You will be using these lines as a guide to cut to on the trim saw. The lines should allow you to cut close to the cab outline but not touch it.

Using the Trim Saw

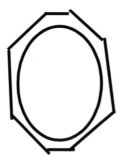

Always use safety glasses when working with the trim saw. The blade uses coarse enough diamond to cause small chips of rock to be thrown from the rock during cutting. Use the 10" trim saw to cut the slab on the trim lines being careful not to cut into the area of the cab. The trim saw uses water with a detergent added as a lubricant and unless you are allergic to dishwater there is no hazard.

Step 2: Grinding the Cab

100 Grit Grind to Mark

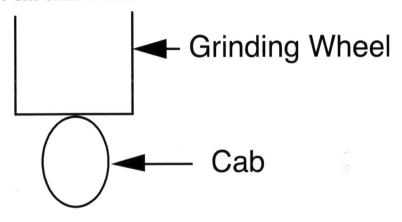

Using the 100 grit diamond grinding belt or wheel, grind the cab to the outline marked on the slab. Check the size frequently with the cab template. The cab should not quite go through the template.

90 Degree Edge

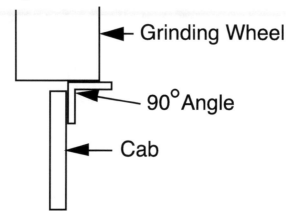

During the grinding process occasionally turn the slab vertically and straighten any angle on the edge back to 90 degrees (square corners).

Step 3: Grinding 15 Deg. Bevel

15 Degree Edge

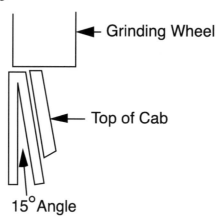

When the cab has been ground to the outline again turn the cab 90 degrees and this time cut a 15 degree bevel sloping toward the top of the cab. The cab should now go about half way through the template.

Step 4: Grinding 45 Deg. Bevel

45 Degree Bevel

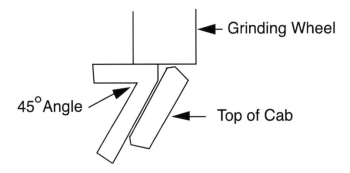

Turn the cab so that the bottom edge is 45 degrees to the grinding wheel and cut a very small (1/32") bevel on the edge. This allows the cab to be set in a finding without cracking.

Step 5: Mark Center, Oval & Side of Cab

Mark Grinding Lines
Using the aluminum rod or marking pen, measure and mark the center

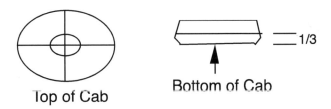

of the top of the cab. Measure and mark an outline of the cab 1/3 the size of the cab on the top. Mark a line around the edge of the cab 1/3 up from the bottom of the cab.

Step 6: Dop the Cab

Dopping
Heat the dop wax in the dop wax heater. The wax should flow but

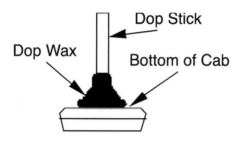

should not boil. A few stones will not tolerate much heat, to cold dop a stone I recommend using double sided carpet tape and a used dop stick with enough dop wax to form a base almost as large as the cab. Some care is required as the tape is not as strong a bond as the wax. Another option is to use a hot glue gun, cyanoacrylic glue, or epoxy.

Heat Stone
Heat the stone on the dop wax heater. The stone should be hot enough to boil a drop of water on its surface.

Mount Stone on Dop Stick
Dip the end of a dop stick in wax. Using tweezers or pliers (the stone is hot) remove the stone from the heat. Place the dop stick on the back of the cab and form the wax around it holding the stick straight. Wet your fingers and use them to center the dop stick on the back of the cab. Place cab and dop stick in water to cool it.

Step 7: Grind Four Side Angles

100 Grit Rough Shape

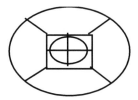

Using the 100 grit grinder, grind a set of flats between the 1/3 grinding lines marked earlier.

Step 8: Grind Cone

100 Grit Cone

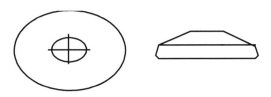

Grind the flats into a cone on the 1/3 grinding lines. Using a rocking motion, grind the cone into the final cab shape.

Step 9: Grind Dome

220 **Grit Final Shape**

Use the 220 fine grinding wheel to smooth the shape and remove all of the rough grinding marks.

Step 10: Sand on 280 Grit
Step 11: Sand on 600 Grit
Step 12: Sand on 1200 Grit
Step 13: Pre-Polish on 3000 Grit

These sanding steps are for the Diamond Pacific Genie and may be slightly different for other brands.
(On the silicon carbide Drums the Grits typically are: 220, 400, and 600)

Sanding
Sanding is the easiest to describe and the hardest to do of all the steps in making a cab. It is also the most important of the steps. Just progress from the coarse grit to the finer grits. At each grit remove all the scratches from the previous step. Clean the cab between each of the silicon carbide belts. It sounds so easy but silicon carbide belts wear relatively fast and a worn 220 grit may be smoother than a new 600 grit. With the finer grits you may need a magnifying glass and a dry stone to see if you have removed all of the previous scratches.

The Funny Travel List Texas: 103 Slang Words, Texas Speak, and Sayin's

A Comical Language Dictionary of the Lone Star State

Chuck Acts

Contents

——

A Special Gift To Our Readers

———

Included in your purchase of this book, we are giving you a fun information book on Texas Slang, Sayings and the History of where they come from. We hope that you like it!

Click on the link below and let us know which email address to deliver it to:

www.funnytravellist.com

Enjoy this book?

Honest reviews of my books are the only thing that helps bring attention of my books to other readers. I don't have the money to throw at advertising. Not yet anyway. So, If you enjoyed this book, I would be grateful if you could spend just 3 minutes leaving a review (It can be as short as you like).

The review button is on the upper left corner of our website. Just scan the code above and look upper left. - Thank you very much.

Facebook Group
WELCOME TO THE GATHERING!

———

If you want to get even more informative insight on Funny Travel Lists, you can always join our Facebook group. Our group includes: Travelers, Boon Dockers, Campers, RV Enthusiast, New Texans and Adventurers. This group was set up to discuss exploring funny and unique places and tell the stories of what we have come across in the US. We are a tight community seeking additional secret adventures while sharing some of our success and failures out on the road. We discuss all types of subjects and many that the general public are unaware! Stop by and see if we have a Funny Travel List book for your state! Be nice and share in the spirit of helping!

The Funny Travel List Group

www.facebook.com/groups/funnytravellist/

Scan the QR code to easily get to the group

The Origins of Texan Speak

———

> *"Texas is a state of mind. Texas is an obsession. Above all, Texas is a*
> *nation in every sense of the word"*
> ***- John Steinbeck (Humphus, n.d.).***

What is Texas slang? Texas slang is a unique dialect that has been developed over time by the people who live in Texas. This dialect includes words and phrases that are not used in other parts of the country, and it can be difficult for outsiders to understand.

So, where does Texas slang come from? The origins of Texas slang can be traced back to the early 1800s when settlers from Texas began moving to other parts of the United States. These settlers brought their unique dialect with them, and it gradually began to spread.

Today, Texas slang is used by people throughout the state, and it continues to evolve over time. Some of the most common expressions include *"y'all," "fixin' to,"* and *"Howdy."*

Before *divin'* in, here are six steps to get *ya'll* started:

1. When *applyin'* Texan, think of words that end in 'g.'

2. Then, don't pronounce that 'g.'

3. Texans love it when you sprinkle the term *"fixin' to"* into dialogue.

4. Don't say "you guys." Refer to *'em* as *"ya'll."*

5. Don't ever call a Coca-Cola a 'pop;' They've got no idea what *ya'll talkin'* about.

6. Congratulations, *ya'll* now versed in Texan speak.

If you're visiting Texas, be sure to brush up on your Texas slang! It will help you to communicate with the locals and get a better understanding of their culture. Happy travels!

Chapter 1:

Texas Slang Words
(Say It With a Twaaaannng)

––––

Ah

This is the Texan version of the word 'I.' It's produced by adding a long twang to the 'I.' Some examples include '*mah*' (my) and '*lahk*' (like).

Ah'ite.

It's the Texan version for the word 'alright.' One example of where it can be used is to provide an affirmative answer when being asked to do something instead of *sayin'* yes.

Bald

The Texas slang term for the word 'boiled.' It's prominent when referring to eggs, "*Would ya like some hardbaldeggs?*"

Big'O

Pronounced "*big-oh*," this is a shortened version of the two words 'big' and 'old.'

Caw

This is the Texan version of 'call' - as in making a phone call. It's typically used in conjunction with the word '*mah*' or '*may*' (meaning me). Put them together, and you've got *cawmay*.

Corn-Fed

Nuttin' to do with maize at all! But rather someone big in stature. This phrase can be used to describe a big boy on the football team.

Double-Backboned

Ya'll can use this term to describe a brave person.

Dun

When *ya'll* completely tired, broken, or desolate, is when this phrase is used. One example is *"I'm dun."*

Gimme

Gimme is a Texan portmanteau of the words "give me." One use case example includes *"Gimme sum lovin'."*

Gonna

A slang term used to say "going to" in Texan speak.

In'thang

The Texan way to any 'anything.'

Jeetjet

It's no secret that food is a significant factor in Texas. So if you want to invite some people to a restaurant, you could ask *"Have ya'll jeetjet?"*

Kicker

This is used for the most compelling reason of pointing something out during an argument or conversation. For example: *"He cheated on her, but here's the kicker…."*

Libel'ta

A phrase used to express the liability of *havin'* to get *sumpin* (something) done. For example, *"She's libel'ta go out and have fun, now that she's single."*

N

This is the Texan way when saying *'than.'* It's predominantly used after a descriptive, such as *"Teacher was madder 'n a wet hen today."*

Nuttin'

The Lone Star state's way of saying 'nothing.' Meaning the word is used in cases such as *"He's got nuttin' on ya."*

O'

This Texan article is placed before the typical English articles 'a' and 'the.' It can be applied to animals and humans. One example includes *"Who's O' good boy?"*

Ov'air

This is how the people in Texas say "over there." For example: *"Where's Scooter gone to now?" "He's ov'air in the barn."*

Piddlee'o

Texans use this phrase to refer to something or someone small. For example, *"That piglet is a piddlee'o thang."*

Place

This phrase is used when *referrin'* to a parcel of property. One example includes *"She's ov'air at Mcdonald place."*

Purt/Purtee

Texans use this slang word to describe *sumpin* as 'pretty' like *'em* other English folks.

R

Use this one on the slight side of caution. Even though pronounced as 'are,' Texans use it as a shortened version for the word 'our.'

Show Nuff

The shortened Texan version of the phrase "sure enough."

Squeat

This slang word is used to shorten the phrase "Let's go eat."

Sumpin

Show nuff by now *ya'll* know this one. But in case *ya* missed it, it's the Texan word for 'something.'

Swate

This is the Texan way of *sayin'* 'sweet.' One use case example includes: "Did *ya'll* say tomorrow's *meetin'* is canceled. *Swate.*"

Tak'n'ta

Yep folks, when there's the need for a family *meetin'*, *ya'll* can say, *"I need to give that boy a tak'n'ta."* It's primarily used when *ya* need to have a stern word with someone.

Thang

This is another one of the first words that'll get stuck in *ya'lls* minds when *attemptin'* to speak Texan. It's their way of *sayin'* 'thing.'

Up'dee

This phrase means being 'insolate' or 'uppity' towards someone. One example of where ya'll can use it includes: *"Pete is being very up'dee with the manager lately."*

Var'mit

This word plays an integral part amongst hunters in Texas. It's used when small animal *huntin'* takes place. For example, *"Tommy and I went var'mit huntin' this morning."*

Wat'nit

This is the way that Texans say, "wasn't it."

Whole'nuther

A Texan term used when one wants to say "a whole other."

Worsh

The Texan word for 'wash.'

Ya'll

It's probably the most famous of all Texas slang terms, provided it's used correctly. It's used to address a group of folks and is the southern contraction of "you all."

Yankee

Texans use this word to refer to any individual originating from the north side of the Red River.

Yer

The way people from Texas say 'your.'

Yonder

Texans use this term to indicate that a person is at another location than they are. For example: "Where's Fort Worth?" "It's yonder in North Texas."

Chapter 2:

Texas *Sayin's*

———

A Fur Piece

Said when *sumpin's* far away, or to indicate a long distance.

All Git Out

A great way to convey that *sumpin* was good or done to the extreme! It can be used to say, *"I went to Blake's house, and his toys were all git out!"*

All Hat, No Cattle

Yep, this one's easy! This is used by a boastful person when they don't really have *anythin'* to brag about anyhow. It's like *talkin'* the talk and not *walkin'* the walk.

"Bless Your Heart"

This phrase is used two-fold. Firstly, you use it to display empathy in a bad situation, and it's also used sarcastically - especially between the ladies.

Bright as a New Penny

Texans use this phrase to describe an intelligent or clever person.

Buzzard Bait

Said of someone or *sumpin* that has died.

Callin' Hogs all Night

A phrase to describe a person or persons that are loud and noisy.

Carryin' Brains in a Pocket

A not-so-nice way to say someone is dumb.

Cattywampus to Miss Jones'

Someone from Texas will use this phrase as a means to say they're confused.

Chin Musician

A Texan term that refers to a talkative person.

"Come Hell or High Water"

This *sayin'* is used when it means that *sumpin'* will be done no matter the cost or what it takes. When a Texan says this, you can be assured of their loyalty.

Cut up Like a Boardin'house Pit

This is said of a person in Texas that is very nervous.

"Dad Gum It"

This is a nice way to replace any swear words when the situation is so dire; Ya'll don't have time to tell the kids to put them earmuffs on.

"Don't Get Ya Panties in a Wad"

This is one way of saying to someone to be more patient.

"Don't Tip Over the Outhouse"

A term used to tell a Texan to be careful or cautious.

Drier 'n Popcorn Fart

A phrase that can be used when the lands are very dry before the rains have *fallin'*, or someone with a very dry sense of humor.

Eatin' Fried Chicken all Week Long

Someone that is financially wealthy.

Expectin' Spoon-Feedin'

A term used to describe someone that is vain in Texas.

Fair to Middlin'

Texans say this when feeling happy and/or good about themselves or a situation they're in.

Flat as a Fritter

A term used to describe a lean or petite person.

First Cousin to Moses Rose

This term is used to describe someone who is shy or timid.

Get/Got on at

This is the Texan phrase for when one has gained employment. It can be used as follows: *"Jesse, got on at Burger King yesterday."*

"Go Cork Yer Pistol"

A nasty comeback used in Texan speak.

Got Caught in His/Her/Their Own Loop

Someone from Texas will use this phrase to imply they've failed at *sumpin*.

Hang Out the Washin'

Said of something or someone that is strong, solid, or robust.

Headin' for the Wagon Yard

A phrase used to say goodbye to someone or announce departure in a conversation.

Hog-Killin' Weather

Texans say this when it's very cold outside.

Hollerin' Down a Well

The Texan way of telling someone that they're wasting time.

Hopper's Busted

Being said of someone that has taken ill.

Hotter 'n Stolen Tamale

This can be said of either the weather or someone that is very good *lookin'*.

Huggin' a Rose Bush

When *sumpin's* deemed as being unacceptable.

"I Could Sit Still for That"

Meanin' sumpin's acceptable to ya.

"I Wasn't Born in Texas, but I Got Here as Fast as I Could"

This is a popular Texas bumper sticker. It means you aren't a Texan native. But that *ya'll* live and breathe every moment Texan-style nonetheless.

"Jumped on Me, Like White on Rice"

A Texan phrase used to say someone is very fast, especially if *ya'll* haven't seen them *comin'*.

Just Fell Off a Turnip/Watermelon/Tater Truck

A term Texans use to refer to an unsophisticated person.

"Know When to Fold 'em"

Yep, a line from the popular Kenny Rogers song, "The Gambler," but it also means that *ya'll* need to know when to call it quits and walk away from a situation or a person.

"Let's Chew the Rag"

Texans use this term to greet someone or before the start of something that needs to be done.

Like a Blister

Said of someone that is very lazy.

Lower Than a Gopher Hole

This is used to describe someone that is feeling very sad.

Might Could

Because *ev'thang* in Texas is *beeg*. The inhabitants of the Lone Star state like to add more words than needed. For instance, this phrase could be used as follows: *"We might could go to the mall today."*

Near About Past Going

When *ya'll* hear someone *sayin'* this, it means they're very tired.

No Hill for a Stepper

Texans use this term to describe sumpin as being easy and requiring little to no effort.

No Pot to Pee in or Window to Throw It Out of

Used when describing someone poor or underprivileged.

One Brick Shy of a Load

Said of a person that is crazy.

Out Where the Buses Don't Run

Said of someone that is desolate and has no place to go.

Ox in a Ditch

This is a way of describing a problem one might have.

Pantin' Like a Lizard on a Hot Rock

This is said of someone that is very busy…with all *sorts'a thangs*.

Pissin' up a Rope

Texans use this term to describe a difficult task or situation.

Pitch a Hissy Fit

Mostly used when kids throw a tantrum. It's also used for adults when someone loses their shit *ish*.

Raised on Concrete

This term is used to describe someone that has been raised in the city or has moved there.

Revolvin' Son of a Bitch

A term used to describe a mean or bad person.

Ridin' a Gravy Train With Biscuit Wheels

Texans use this term to describe a person with a lot of luck.

Sandpapered

Texans would say this when they've been defeated by something or someone.

Screwworm

Said of an unwelcome person in Texas.

Short Arms and Deep Pockets

A Texas term used to describe a cheap or stingy person.

Slicker 'n Slop Jar

Nuttin' to do with someone *bein'* messy, but rather refers to a dishonest person.

Sittin' on a Nest

A way to describe a pregnant woman.

Suckin' the Hind Teat

Said of a useless or inept person or situation.

"The Barn Door's Open and the Mule's Tryin' to Get Out"

Lol! Probably one of the best ways to say the cucumber has left the salad, i.e., mate, ya fly is down!

"The Only Hell His/Her Mama Ever Raised"

A very Texan way of *sayin'* someone's real mad or argumentative. Also, a nicer way to say someone is hot-headed.

"This Ain't My First Rodeo"

When someone says this, they're tryin' to say that they are either capable or experienced in a matter.

Throw Your Hat O'er the Windmill

This is one Texan way to say it's time to celebrate.

Tighter 'n Bark on a Log

Texans use this term to describe a drunk or intoxicated person.

"You Can Take That to the Bank"

Meanin' something is true and can also be used to describe an honest person.

Wide as Two Ax Handles

Rude as it might be (to those in the know), this is one way of *sayin'* someone's overweight.

Wilder 'n Acre of Snakes

This phrase is used to describe a 'loose' or immoral person.

Wouldn't Cut Hot Butter

Someone or something very dull.

A Special Gift To Our Readers

—

Included in your purchase of this book, we are giving you a fun information book on Texas Slang, Sayings and the History of where they come from. We hope that you like it!

Click on the link below and let us know which email address to deliver it to:

www.funnytravellist.com

Enjoy this book?

Honest reviews of my books are the only thing that helps bring attention of my books to other readers. I don't have the money to throw at advertising. Not yet anyway. So, If you enjoyed this book, I would be grateful if you could spend just 3 minutes leaving a review (It can be as short as you like).

The review button is on the upper left corner of our website. Just scan the code above and look upper left. - Thank you very much.

Facebook Group
WELCOME TO THE GATHERING!

———

If you want to get even more informative insight on Funny Travel Lists, you can always join our Facebook group. Our group includes: Travelers, Boon Dockers, Campers, RV Enthusiast, New Texans and Adventurers. This group was set up to discuss exploring funny and unique places and tell the stories of what we have come across in the US. We are a tight community seeking additional secret adventures while sharing some of our success and failures out on the road. We discuss all types of subjects and many that the general public are unaware! Stop by and see if we have a Funny Travel List book for your state! Be nice and share in the spirit of helping!

The Funny Travel List Group

www.facebook.com/groups/funnytravellist/

Scan the QR code to easily get to the group

References

———

Dingus, A. (1994, December 1). *More colorful Texas sayings than you can shake a stick at.* TexasMonthly. https://www.texasmonthly.com/being-texan/more-colorful-texas-sayings-than-you-can-shake-a-stick-at/

Enchanting Texas. (2022, January 11). *28 famous Texas quotes and Texas sayings.* Enchanting Texas. https://enchantingtexas.com/texas-quotes-sayings/

Humphus, B. (n.d.). *15 Texas sayings ideas | Texas, Texas quotes, loving Texas.* Pinterest. https://za.pinterest.com/bhumphus/texas-sayings/

Norton, K. (n.d.). *30 things people from Texas have to explain to out-of-towners.* Movoto. https://www.movoto.com/guide/tx/things-people-from-texas-have-to-explain/

Ray, D. (n.d.). *Texas dialect | Words, Texas, phrase.* Pinterest. https://za.pinterest.com/pin/AcJ1ho2z14UUJlaGw9NohNLDVSsOoGaDqpufifXgmCFq-p6FxeuBAeE/

UStravelia. (2014, December 22). *118 famous Texas sayings and phrases along with their meanings.* UStravelia. https://ustravelia.com/famous-texas-sayings-phrases

Made in the USA
Monee, IL
14 June 2022

Diamond is easier to see the scratch removal, a worn diamond does not get finer just slower. With any belt you may find it easier to remove all the previous scratches if the last step on each belt is to sand in only one direction. Then when you are looking for scratches any that are going in that direction are scratches that have not yet been removed and you are not yet ready to go on to the next belt. Silicon carbide has another characteristic that can irritate you. The grit can come loose from a worn belt leaving a deep scratch in the cab that may require going back to a coarser belt to remove.

Pre-polish
Finish sanding on the 3000 grit diamond wheel. A well worn 600 silicon carbide is about a 1000 grit and will pre-polish adequately.

Step 14: Polishing the Cab

Cerium Oxide
Cerium oxide is the polish of choice for agate and most other silicon dioxide based material (opal, obsidian, quartz, glass, etc.). Cerium oxide is usually mixed about ten to one with water and applied by spraying from a spray bottle, painting with a small brush, or squeezing from a squeeze bottle on its leather buff (do not mix polishes on the buffs) and hold the cab against the buff using a tight grip on the dop stick and a fair amount of pressure. The cab should "pull" against the buff as the polish dries and polishing takes place. Spray more oxide as the buff dries. The agate will get warm in the polishing process, be careful not to let it get hot enough to melt the dop wax. Agate should polish in one or two minutes.

Other Polishes

Tin Oxide
Used the same way as cerium oxide but works better on softer stones, turquoise for example.

Diamond

Comes in four forms, bort, belts, paste and sprays. 3M makes a 3000 and 50,000 belt set that is excellent for jade or any stone that has a tendency to undercut. Paste and sprays are cheaper but are harder to work with.

ZAM

Used on a canvas wheel, Zam is used on soft stones like lower grade turquoise and plastics (reconstructed stones).

Chrome Oxide

Mixed with vinegar, chrome oxide is preferred by many as a polish for jade.

Aluminum Oxide

Aluminum oxide is a good general purpose polish. It has the advantage of being sold in a variety of forms and many different grits. It tends to be a little more expensive than most of the other oxides but if you are having a problem getting a stone to polish with the cheaper oxides, you might want give this a try. It will work on almost all hardnesses of stones.

Others

There are several other polishes sold under various trade names and many people swear by them, others at them. After you are familiar with the standards feel free to experiment. You may find one that works better for you.

Remove from Dop Stick

Refrigerate

If a freezer is available, remove the cab from the dop stick by placing them in the freezer for a short time. When they are frozen the cab will almost fall off the stick. Ice cubes in water will also work.

Heat or Knife

If a freezer is not available the wax can be heated over the burner until the wax is soft enough to allow the cab to be pried off. Any remaining wax can be removed with a knife. The dop wax may also be dissolved with alcohol.

Stone Setting

Commercial Settings

As a beginner you will probably want to buy your first setting (called "findings"), later on you may want to consider making your own "findings". Commercial findings generally use one of two ways to set the stone, prongs or bezel.

Prongs

Prongs are small metal "fingers" that are bent around the edge of the stone to hold it in place. Using a small hammer and a hard wood rod as a "pusher," carefully pound the prongs down over the cab a little at a time working on opposite prongs until the cab is held firmly.

Bezels

Bezels are a strip of thin metal running around the stone with the stone just fitting inside the strip. The metal is pushed down all around the stone compressing the metal as it is pushed until the stone is firmly held in place. Using a small hammer and a polished metal "pusher," work around the cab alternating sides until the bezel has a scalloped look. Continue alternating sides between the scallops until the bezel is flat. Use a burnishing tool to remove any marks that are left.

Common Stones Used in Cabs

Type of Stones

Natural stones commonly used to make cabs include: agate, quartz, jasper, jade, turquoise, magnesite, opal, obsidian, and malachite. The first three are hard enough to be used in almost any finding including mens' belt buckles (men tend to scratch buckles no matter what is in them). The others are softer and their suitability for use may depend on who is going to wear it and where.

There are other stones commonly in use for cabs that are man-made: reconstructed, stabilized, goldstone, triplets, Gilson, and Victoria Stone.

Reconstructed stones, usually turquoise or malachite but there are several others, are made by grinding lower grade material into a powder and mixing it with a type of epoxy. It is easy to work with and there is a minimum of waste material but it can be hard to polish, it is as soft as plastic. However some are very attractive.

Most of the turquoise that is available today has been stabilized. High quality natural turquoise is relatively rare and if any good, very expensive. In recent years the stabilization process has improved a lot and unless you want natural for aesthetic reasons I wouldn't hesitate to use stabilized turquoise. In the stabilization process the rough turquoise is impregnated with an epoxy-like plasticizer. Depending on the process, this can produce a very hard attractive stone. It also has the advantage of not absorbing skin oil which can cause natural turquoise to change color.

Goldstone is glass that has had finely ground metal particles added to make it glitter. It is normally found in gold or blue, and rarely in green.

Triplets are usually made by starting with a black backing to which a paper-thin piece of precious opal is glued. Then a clear quartz cap is glued on top. These can be very beautiful and relatively expensive.

Gilson is a French manufacturer that specializes in creating synthetic stones for the jewelry market. His stones include turquoise, opal, and emerald. They are well made and can be very expensive. I think Gilson is no longer being manufactured but Chatham and at least one Japanese company have the patents and are making emeralds and opals, I have not seen any of this type of turquoise in many years.

Victoria Stone is a man-grown material that has no real equivalent in nature. It comes in many colors and has a chatoyant pattern that many find very attractive. It is no longer made; the inventor passed away and took the formula to the grave with him. You still see it occasionally as slabs or finished stones at Gem Shows or on the Web.

There are other man-made materials and new ones showing up regularly. Just when you think you have seen them all someone will show you something new. It keeps the hobby interesting.

Most materials are available at local Lapidary Shops (Rock Shops) or shows, all are available on the Web.

Other Shapes

Square
Square cabs are most commonly found in mens' rings.

Round
Round cabs require time and patience. The eye can see small imperfections that would be overlooked in an oval.

Oval
The oval is the most common shape. It has the advantage that the eye will forgive small shape imperfections.

Hearts
Hearts are frequently used for pendants. They are usually cut double-sided and patience is required for the notch.

Where to Buy Materials

Club Shows
Club shows are one of the most interesting places to buy materials. There are usually several dealers selected to cover different areas of the hobby, and displays of local and regional lapidary work. The displays are a wealth of ideas and you will meet many wonderful people. Look for some local shows on the Web.

http://www.rockhounds.com/
http://www.amfed.org/

These two Web sites are a good place to start looking. The first has a list of many Club shows and the second has information on the several U. S. federations which will each have lists of local clubs and local shows.

Websites List
https://www.lascodiamond.com/products/index.htm
http://www.lopacki.com/
http://www.riogrande.com/
http://www.ameritool-inc.com/
http://www.sfjssantafe.com/
http://www.micromark.com/
http://www.mtmist.org/
http://www.kingsleynorth.com/
http://lortone.com/
http://www.rockhounds.com/graves/
http://www.diamondpacific.com/
http://www.eastwindabrasive.com/
http://www.ijsinc.com/
http://www.foredom.com/
http://www.jadecarver.com/
http://www.harmons.net/

This is just short list of available Web sites, there are hundreds and they are constantly changing, new ones starting up, old ones dropping off, and content and supplies changing on current ones.

Other Lapidary Arts

There are several more fields of interest in the lapidary hobby, some have been touched on already. Most people have interests that cover more than one of these.

Tumblers

Many times the starting place for the beginner is a tumbler, polishing up stones they have collected. Sometimes this interest is expanded into making tumbled stone necklaces or other artful endeavors.

There are two types of tumblers, rotary, and vibrating. Rotary tumblers are less expensive, at least small ones, and are usually what people start with. They are easy to use and will normally give reasonable results but they are noisy and take a long time, sometimes several weeks, to finish each batch. Some people, especially young children, loose interest before they are done.

Vibrating tumblers are more expensive but take less time to finish each batch. Sometimes just a few days. That makes it easier to keep interested in the process.

In general rotary tumblers will produce a more rounded stone, while vibrating tumblers will leave more of the original rough stone shape. Some people prefer one, where as, some the other.

With some practice both will produce an acceptable result. Although, it can take more time and study to produce really good results than many people realize.

Faceting

Diamonds are the stones most people think of first when faceted stones are mentioned but faceting diamond is almost never done by the hobbyist. The equipment is too specialized, the experience required too great, and the cost too high. But almost any other stone can be (and has been) faceted by the hobbyist, although normally only transparent or translucent stones are used. The equipment is not cheap but it is affordable, and although there is a lot of experience required for a good stone, most anyone with enough patience can do it.

Many clubs have members that facet and will teach other members to do it. Some Community Colleges have adult classes that include faceting, many times taught by the same people that teach it in the local clubs. If you are interested in learning to facet these sources are a good place to start.

Some people go to a Dealer that sells faceting machines and buy one thinking, correctly, that they will come with instructions. These instructions, although correct, rarely are intended for a beginner and many times are the reason for an almost new machine being sold.

Carving

People are all familiar with the large carvings like Mount Rushmore, the ancient Greek statues, and the small Chinese figurines. But there are so many different materials, each with its own hardness, carving technique and tools that there is something for anyone who wants to try the art.

It is possible that the art of carving something from nature to wear as jewelry predates the human use of fire. If true, that would make it one of the earliest forms of art. Certainly primitive man had the capability to pick up a pretty shell and grind a hole in it with a sharp rock and wear it as a decoration. I have seen garnet beads with holes ground in them, made by American Indians before the White Man came.

Jewelry carving, as we know it started about 5000 years ago, when the Chinese invented the treadle. They used a foot pedal to supply the power to turn a flywheel which then turned a wooden rod that had a hole drilled in one end. In the hole, they inserted a small wooded stick, many times a piece of bamboo. They used a mixture of ground sand and water to grind small, and sometimes not so small, statues and jewelry adornments.

After 5000 years we still have not found a better way to do it, we just have better tools to do it.

Some clubs have the instructors and tools to teach carving. There are not as many people doing carving as faceting so finding instructions from someone to show you how get started is a little harder. But if you are interested, look around, there are a few books, a few clubs, and Community Colleges that do teach it and the results can be spectacular.

Beading
Beading has recently enjoyed a renewed interest and a whole culture has grown up around the art. There are stores, clubs, and shows devoted to beading. If this is one of your interests there are many magazines devoted to the hobby. Most of the local clubs have members who are interested in beading.

Intarsia (Inlay)
Intarsia is the art of cutting different colored stones into shapes that will then be pieced together into scenes. It is time consuming work but the results can be incredible. Stained glass could be considered a variant of intarsia although it is usually not done by the same people.

Specimen Collecting
People collect all sorts of lapidary items: minerals, crystals, slabs, geodes, picture scenes, flats, fossils, fluorescents, and many others. They are frequently displayed at home or in display cases at local club shows

and libraries. Some collections are good enough to be loaned to museums.

Silver and Gold Smithing

After you have cut your first few cabs you are faced with the question of what to do with them. You can mount them in factory-made findings or you can display them in a display case, but most people want something more. Silver and gold smithing can be roughly divided into two general categories: fabrication and casting.

Fabrication is the art of working with metal directly, hammering, sawing, soldering, etc. Casting is the art of working with a secondary medium, usually wax, and then converting the secondary medium to metal.

Made in the USA
Monee, IL
14 June 2022